Anybody Can Be A Nobody Why Not Be A Somebody

Kaleb Cloyd

Anyone Can Be A Nobody, Why Not Be a Somebody

Copyright © 2018 Kaleb Cloyd

All rights reserved under International and Pan-American Copyright Conventions

No part of this book may be reproduced, stored in a retrieval system or transmitted in any way by any means, electronic, mechanical, photocopy, recording or otherwise without the prior permission of the author except as provided by USA copyright law.

ISBN-13: 978-0578-43362-2

Contents

Preface	v
About the Author	vii
Introduction	ix
1 In the Driver's Seat	1
2 Seeing Every Opportunity	7
3 Work Harder than Ever	11
4 How to Persuade	15
5 Clique, Gossips and Complainers	23
6 Training for Success	29
7 Examples of Humility	33
8 Stuck in Neutral	39
9 Should you go alone?	47
10 Respect Along the Way	51

Preface

Anyone can say words; but it takes action to get a job done.

Anyone can go from being a "nobody" to being "somebody."

Are you ready to be somebody?

About the Author

Kaleb Cloyd is the founder and CEO of *Kaleb's Fundamentals*: A Strategic Education Consulting Business. During the last 7 years, Kaleb has been in Sales, both in the *Fitness Industry* and in the *Automotive Industry*. He has worked for **Hyundai, Kia, Chevrolet,** and **Ford Motor Company**. Kaleb is also an accomplished *Public Speaker*, winning 3 Awards. In 2016, he began investing in *Real Estate*, starting **Kaleb Cloyd Properties, LLC.** Kaleb holds certifications from **Chevrolet Automotive** and**Ford Motor Company, Honda,** as well as a certificate in *Day Trading* from **Trading University**, and a certificate in *Nutrition*. Kaleb now spends his time helping people achieve their purpose through **Kaleb's Fundamentals**.

Introduction

Are you on board?

I'm Kaleb. I was born in Dallas, where life was pretty simple for me. In middle school and high school, I was very good at sports, got along with everyone, and was looked up to for my character. In business, I've achieved many rewards and have been very successful. Now, I want to teach others what I know to help them in their pursuit of personal success.

When you are on your way to be successful in life, it starts out like driving an automobile.

What are your goals?

How will you achieve them?

What are you good at?

What life stage are you in?

Do you take the passenger-seat approach to life, or do you jump into the driver's seat?

I used the example of the automobile because an automobile takes you where you want and need to go. What vehicle are you using to be successful?

CHAPTER 1

IN THE DRIVER'S SEAT

In an automobile, there are certain gauges that tell how fast you are going; those with global navigation can tell you where you are going. In life, you need to know *where* you're going. You may be reading this book while sitting in the passenger seat of life.

It is time for you to get in the driver's seat.

Imagine you are driving in this situation. You are on one of your first sales assignments in a new job. Driving is a vital part of your job and the way you live. As a result of your good driving record and the respect you show people on the road, you have great opportunities to get ahead. How hard do you think you will have to work to remain a safe driver? Why should you maintain self-control, even in difficult situations?

When you are driving you have to be aware of where you are going, In your journey toward success there are many roadways that you can take. The driving task in life is going to include all the skilled actions you must take. You will need to know how to make decisions in your life. Decision- making skills is mainly a mental, You will have to know when to slow and to go. Deciding when and where to steer your life, Is very important. In this chapter I want you to picture yourself in an automobile in the driver. In the journey you need to know these four things

1. Identify where you're going.

2. Know what you're going to do.

3. Know when to accelerate and when to brake.

4. Execute on reaching your destination (getting the job done).

Adjusting the Controls

You have a responsibility to seek financial freedom. You also have a responsibility to control your attitude. Your attitude affects your willingness to learn. Your attitude can have a major influence on where you are heading in your life. Some people confuse getting attention or showing off with gaining recognition—confusing it with success. Some people go fast and recklessly to get attention. Their idea of a good time might be to scare other people. Conversely, some people deliberately make respectful choices day in and day out, year after year. Over time, they earn the respect of others by being a good role model or example in all circumstances.

Your ability to manage your relationships with others. At times people you know might try to get you to do things you normally would not do. In the journey of knowing where you are going, you need to be eager to learn in the process. You will have challenges on the road to success. You will learn that as a result of your knowledge, attitude and expertise, you become more efficient and effective.

To start out right there is a decision-making process which you will start identifying every day. As you go you will be influenced by your attitude on what you know about your journey. On your journey there will be guidelines that you will probably notice from people that will give you thoughts and ideas about been on the path toward whether it is that you want to succeed in.

One on the questions you need to ask yourself is this: Are you prepared to be successful? What you are going to need is self-education and mental preparation. Once you are prepared mentally, you need to start making progress. You'll learn more as you proceed. Another question to consider is this: How will you stay motivated so that you won't give up?

It is important to take control of your life to be successful. Developing control involves visual habits. In life – just like when driving – you need to develop the ability to analyze situations. Developing good habits is important for when challenging situations occur. You need to identify clues that can lead to the correct outcome. Your task is to think. You begin by visually searching the situation to get information for your next decision. You quickly develop the skills to know when to search, where to search and how to search. Different environments and situations present a variety of visual search problems. As you gain experience, you will learn what kinds of situations and events are most important to identify.

Along the way you might be sharing the journey with someone else. Would this be a problem for you?

Where should you evaluate the journey if someone is on a similar journey just like you? As you go on the road to success you will meet people. You might even have to maneuver around them to get where you want to go.

On the Road to Success

When entering the road of success make sure you have the right guidelines. It is easy to make a mistake if you do not have the correct information. You must evaluate yourself and know which route is best for you. When you enter the road, be alert for others who may try to stop you. When this happens, you may have to adjust. When you see situations like this come toward you, keep a long-distance view to avoid conflict. One roadblock can be other people's intentions. If you are not sure of another person's intentions, you might want to steer around them.

How good can you see? Most information you will gather is by your ability to see. You must be able to see clearly and quickly to be safe and responsible. You must be able to read to identify what's coming toward you. You must recognize the distance between yourself and others.

I want to briefly mention emotions. Emotions influence the way you think and act. When emotions affect your thoughts and actions, you must be careful. Strong emotions can interfere with your ability to think and reason. Your chances of making a mistake increase. The effect that an emotion has on your ability to go depends upon the strength of the emotion and the effort you make to resist the effect of it.

Let's talk about keeping yourself in good condition so you will not get burned out. Learning about yourself can help give you confidence to handle problems as they come. You need to know yourself.

Preparation is what you must do because you will be going to places. If you are successful in preparation, things will go the way you want them to go.

Through this book, I will be talking about the work environment and what goes on inside jobs, offering advice on what to do and how to respond.

CHAPTER 2

SEEING EVERY OPPORTUNITY

Oftentimes in life we pass on opportunities because we make excuses. When a person is getting off work, there is always time left, but we make excuses. I do not have an enough time or it's too late. Sometimes we miss the most important things in our lives because we do not realize the opportunity factor. Investing can play a factor as well. If we know about "investing" then we would see opportunities better. I met this lady one time who was going to school to learn about real estate. I myself was already in real estate as an investor. I told her that, I go to real estate seminars and so invited her to go. She was ready to go but the day before the seminar she did not want to go. She had a choice that could have changed her life; perhaps she could have saved time or money by attending the seminar.

When you first start working, you should already be looking for more work because you must prepare your future. Ask yourself what I will be doing 5 years from now and how I will get there.

One thing about life is that there is uncertainty. Sometimes you just will not know what will happen especially at your job. A person must learn to be an observer of what is going on around them. Try looking out for yourself while you are working.

The problem is that many times we do not recognize an opportunity when it comes along. Opportunities can come in the form of salesmen. They knock on are door, but we do not want to open it. Opportunities come in many ways and sometimes its unexpected. People are so caught in distractions and miss most opportunities.

The word opportunity comes from the Latin term "opportunitas," which is composed of two others meaning forward and portus, "port.". This word came about from navigation where sailors used the phrase portus to denote the best combination of currents and tides to sail to various ports. The only way to seize such weather conditions was if the captain had already sighted the port of destination. Knowing the weather conditions without knowing where you want to go is useless. Therefore, a ship was in state of "opportunitas" when its captain had decided where to go and knew how to get there.

Sometimes when people pass on opportunities, adversity comes. What kind of adversity is it? It may take some time to accept that it's a part of our life that may change on how you define yourself. One step you can take is to prepare yourself mentally. Embrace the perspective your situation provides, whether you have been hurt. Take advantage by looking for something productive. Starting a support group for other people that had similar experience to your own. Reframing from adversity in your mind is start. Embrace the experience adversity provides you. The difference between someone that can handle anything and somebody that cannot is often that one has already been through it.

CHAPTER 3

Work Harder than Ever

What does it mean to "work hard"? What does "working hard" look like? The term "working hard" has been tossed around so much that it seems to have a watered-down meaning. Here are my ideas that define "working hard."

Learning to Soar

If you want work hard, you need to zoom pass mediocrity to pursue the excellence that is ahead of you. You must stop grubbing for worms or scratching for bugs like a pen full of chickens. You must learn to soar like a powerful eagle. You must live above the base level of mediocrity and refuse to let the majority shape your standard.

Soaring may look easy for the eagle; but, for those of us without wings, it takes a strong mental effort made of clear, courageous and confident thinking. Very few people ooze their way out of mediocrity. It takes pressure and force to pursue excellence and win battles.

Conquering Mediocrity

How can I as A person who has many years of mediocrity thinking change. If you are serious about conquering mediocrity! You need to reconstruct your thinking. Begin this process of mental discipline: think thoughts of excellence! Instead of telling yourself that you are a helpless victim, take charge of those thoughts! As soon as you catch yourself responding negatively or defensively, stop and analyze the situation. Consider a positive way to respond; consider your situation; consider your future. People who soar are those who exercise clear, courageous and confident thinking.

Being Flexible

By having flexibility, you can take advantage of unexpected opportunities when they come your way. You may sometimes consider quitting one job to go with another company where your chances for advancement might be better. But, is that true?

Would a new job really increase your chances of reaching your goals?

Does the new company promote from within or hire from outside to fill the best jobs?

Would you fit in with new set of coworkers?

What other affects will changing jobs have on your schedule, family, other expenses?

Sometimes taking a new job with another company may be the best thing; other times, it's not. Stay flexible so you can identify the best opportunities.

Adopting Adaptability

Can you learn to do different things? Are you willing to do things that might push you out of your comfort zone? This can mean you are adaptable, and it is a highly sought trait. If you are ready to try something new, you need to let your boss know. Your employer expects you to do whatever needs to be done and will likely be glad to let you tackle something new.

Remember, cooperation with others is a great trait, too. If you are looking for a promotion, cooperation is necessary. Cooperation and adaptability go hand-in-hand.

When you are working hard, have an attitude to see past the majority. Everything we deal with in life begins in the mind. Living differently should clear the mental fog. Innovation replaces mental resistance. Determination marches in overstepping.

Work vs. Career vs. Job

Work, career and job are words that sometimes are confused. We will look at the meaning of these words. "Work" is an activity that produces something of value. Those who work are usually paid for it, but not always. For example, some do volunteer work and receive no pay.

Work consistently performed over a number of years is known as a career. When I talk with people about "work," they often think of a "career."

"Job" simply refers to employment. When you think about your life, do you think about your work as having an effect on your lifestyle? More than half of the working person's waking hours are spent on work. Therefore, it's important to consider the effect you want your work to have on your lifestyle.

Develop your aspiration while you are working. What is the aspiration? Aspiration defines you along your journey. It is *why* you do what you do. It motivates *how* you do what you do. It's how you want to be remembered. To be successful, you need to determine what it is that you want to be successful doing and then determine how to achieve that.

CHAPTER 4

How to Persuade

Cooperation from others is one of the major factors of success, no matter what kind of work you do. One of the first things a person can learn when he goes to work is that all business is a cooperative environment. You must cooperate with someone and offer to do something for him if you want him to cooperate with you.

It simply comes down to this: If you want to gain cooperation and full support, then you need first to give your cooperation and support. They will be interested in cooperating with you and supporting you as well. Warning: If you're not giving your coworkers your complete cooperation and full support, they can tell that quite easily.

If you want to persuade people to support you and cooperate with you, you must win their confidence. The best way to do this is to always tell the whole truth.

Developing Truthfulness

1. Be honest and truthful at all times. If you can't say anything good to another person, then do not say anything.

2. Make your word your bond. If you want people to have full confidence in you, then you must keep your word. Every time.

The Value of a Witness

The most important thing a trial lawyer can do is to present witnesses. The judge and jury may think that the lawyer is prejudiced in his/her views in support of his/her client. So, the attorney must prove his/her case to win the confidence and support of the jury. He does this by calling his witnesses to the stand to verify that what he says is true.

You also can use "witnesses" to persuade people and to establish the confidence of others in what you say and do. It's the most reliable way of doing business.

Playing on a Team

If you want people to support you, be part of a team. Are you willing to share the same hardships, the same discomforts? Simple cooperation like this will establish a bond that is hard to forge in any other way.

Getting Along with Your Boss

To get ahead in the business world, it's really important to establish a cordial and honest working relationship with your boss. To have the opportunity to "get to the top and stay there," you must get along with your superior.

To accomplish this, there are a few respect-building things that managers look for in their employees:

1. Be known as a hard worker. Nothing makes an employer happier than seeing an employee toiling away at the job: looking busy, sounding busy, *being* busy.

2. Recognize and communicate according to his/her strengths. For example, if she works at a rapid-fire pace, then offer short, concise updates stated briefly and without embellishment. If she wants all the details, then report them . Presenting an idea to your boss successfully depends on the words you use and the preparation and research you do before meeting. So, you must know what you are going to talk about and how you're going to present your ideas.

3. Be prepared. Know your subject inside and out, backward and forward. Be prepared to make decisions when your boss asks for your recommendations. Don't ask him to make your decisions for you: he has enough problems of his own to solve. Don't miss this: Your

boss will appreciate you much more if you recommend decisions that he can support. Know all the details of your proposition. Be prepared to answer any question. Propose decisions he/she can support. And, above all, be courteous when presenting your idea.

Correcting a Colleague without Ruining the Relationship

I want to talk to you about how to correct someone's mistakes without ruining a friendship. If you cannot use criticism properly you might not be able to correct the mistake. When you can correct a person's mistakes without criticizing him for making them you will see a difference. The people that look up to you will do a far better job for you. They won't make the same mistake twice in a row. People will work with initiative, ingenuity and enthusiasm. They will be motivated to do their best. You will make them feel important when you do not tear them part for his or her mistakes.

Selling Yourself

You may not realize this, but there are certain things you do in this life that will require salesmanship. If you are not in sales work this is a good way to learn by seeing yourself as a sales person. You can apply salesmanship in your social life. When you ask your friends if they want to hangout, if they say yes you persuaded them in one way. If people get along with you, you probably use persuasion very good. One way to persuade people is to build rapport with them first then you can convince them easily. I have had a lot of success persuading business associates because I build rapport with them. Another way to persuade is to become social. This might be out of the comfort zone for some people. You must be confident to go up to people and talk to them. Once you add a little bit of social personality to your life, being shy will become less of a hindrance for you. You can practice this every day. Working at jobs that required me to sell helped me to overcome shyness and become more social; it also helped me build my communication skills. Start putting yourself in front of people and stop being shy.

Here's a real-life example of how I started to overcome shyness. I worked at a gym and people would try to sneak in without a membership. I desperately wanted to avoid conflict. I didn't want to tell them that they can't work out because they don't have a membership. But, one day I started developing mental stuffiness and started telling people that tried to sneak into the gym that they must have a membership to work out. There were situations where I had to make a decision that required me to be upfront with people and speak the truth even if they (we) did not like it. I had to be tough.

Motivating Others

When people start to notice your initiative, you will probably start motivating people around you–even your coworkers and your boss. The teacher, like the team leader, is often a disguised role. You may not teach in school, but you've probably shared your knowledge of something with others. Teaching can be frustrating. Although you can easily perform a skill yourself, you might find yourself perplexed when trying to get someone else to do it correctly.

It's okay to point out progress as it occurs. In the early stages of learning, recognize effort and results. If your employees accomplish everything you teach them, your standards are too low. Require everyone to make quality contributions regularly. Employees and employers should ask each other questions. You can start off by asking your boss: What questions do you have for me? The employer also has a responsibility to ask questions to reduce any possible failures.

Sometimes, the most difficult people to motivate can be your colleagues. They are parallel in position to you and, therefore, are not compelled to take orders from you. The key to motivating your colleagues is to convince them that you have something they need–and that you are willing to share it with them. In return, you'll listen to their ideas as they contribute with equal value. Great ideas attract great minds. Remember: having a reputation for consistently getting the job done attracts quality people to you.

You can create empathy among your colleagues by relating your needs in a meaningful way. Show your willingness to do your part. Try to find ways to motivate them for success in the areas they value you most. Ask for advice; as this shows them that you value their input. If you are consistently associated with getting things done people will notice.

If you are in management, you must know how to keep employees. Here are some reasons why employees stay at their jobs:

1. Receive good pay

2. Have a mentor

3. Feel valued

4. Shown appreciation

5. Been empowered

Some employees are there only to work. The average worker just wants to make enough to get by. Then you have workers that are excellent at what they do. They do more than what is required of them. They want to be promoted. If you are a manager, you need to find out why employees want to work for you. Sometimes, if you do not give them attention, they won't give you any attention.

The best way to teach being responsible is to give them responsibility. Do not boss your employees around. Instead, management needs to have sustaining motivation to pass along to employees. Motivation should be reignited regularly.

If you are the employee, take the initiative to learn from your management. Employees should pursue special opportunities that result in areas of development for the company. Sometimes management does not give clear guidelines for employee development; if not, take initiative and ask.

Other tips for being an employee that motivates others and gets the attention of management include:

- Take the initiative to find the work that needs to be done.

- Learn the company's policies and procedures; read the employee handbook.

- Show eagerness to learn everything you can about your job.

- Be dependable, be on time, never make them wonder where you are.

The best employees are those who like their work and are enthusiastic about it. Find the part of your job that is most interesting to you, so you can show enthusiasm for it.

CHAPTER 5

Clique, Gossips and Complainers

Let's talk about cliques. The clique refers to a group of people; but, not all groups are cliques. They tend to leave some people out of the loop. How is a clique formed? They can be formed by people who have similar mindsets or share common interests, but sometimes it is not for the good. If you work, then you need to watch out for this. It is important to hang around good influences. People will either pull you up or pull you down. Two attributes you will find in a clique are gossip and negativity. They will talk bad about employees. They will talk bad management and complain about things.

What you must do is surround yourself with positive people and to remember if you get caught in gossip it can back to get you. I am been in sales for a long time. I surround myself with positive coworkers. It has made a difference in my life. Here is why it's bad to have cliques at work: they thrive when no one addresses their behavior. They will bully you. Cliques often focus on maintaining their popularity and making you feel less important. Jealously can be found among them, too.

Here is how to stop a clique from forming: If you're a boss, do not assign the same people to the same tasks all the time. Instead of forming a clique, form a squad. A squad is a group of people that are assembled for a specific task.

As an employee, find out what kind of person you are. Then, seek a common goal that you and your coworkers can talk about. Find coworkers that want to help others. There will be times when you will have to stick to yourself before you decide who to talk to. Do not say too much to people you barely know – especially anything that is personal. Keep it professional until you've had some time to build trust.

So, in a squad, you are on a mission to help people.

Having the right friends is as important. If you're having trouble deciding whether you have a good friend or not then your relationship may be already on rocks. Friends should offer support and make you feel needed and confident. Friends should not gossip. If yours gossips a lot, then it's likely that your friend is gossiping about you when you are not around. Friends should stay true to their words. If your friends never seem to do what they say they would do, they are not keeping their word. Take the time to reflect on why your friends might want to hang out with you. Do you make them feel good? Your friends should make you feel good about yourself, too.

Gossip occurs in almost every workplace. Gossip has been misunderstood for a long time. So, let's first determine what gossip is. The Hebrew term for speaking badly of others is "lashon hara," literally meaning "evil." It is very malicious. The best way to avoid gossip is to not open your mouth.

Here are examples of what is and what isn't gossip. One of your coworkers is late for work and you tell your boss he/she is late. That is not gossip. But, if you start speaking badly of his/her character pertaining to why he/she is late to work, and you tell your boss, that results in gossip.

If you are in management, do not invite gossip. Set a good example for your employees. If you need to improve in this area as a manager, then just stop gossiping. Walk away when you are tempted. Don't open your mouth. And, regarding gossip, listen to your employees who report it–and stop it in its tracks.

As employees who want to curb gossip:

1. Avoid gathering places for gossip

2. Change the subject when gossip starts

3. Approach your management team when you hear gossip

4. Act professionally

The Problem with Complainers

Do yourself a favor and don't hang around complainers. Complainers want people to join their pity parties so that they can feel better about themselves. It's easy to feel pressured into listening to complainers because you don't want to be callous. There is a fine line between lending a sympathetic ear and getting drawn into their negative emotional spiral. Negative thinking can damage the neural structure that regulates emotions. It can cause brain disruptions.

If you are the complainer, then consider that your attitude needs to change toward people and yourself. Your attitude either attracts people or repels people. If you have a negative attitude and are not willing learn or take advice, you probably won't be successful.

Steps to avoid complainers:

1. Remove yourself from people and things that distract you.

2. Stay away from people that "play the victim" and don't accept any responsibility.

3. Stay away from people that think they know it all. They don't.

4. Stay away from drama. It leads to exaggerations and gossip.

Clique, Gossips and Complainers

Have you ever told somebody to do something and they said they would do it but never do? Have you ever been given information that was not right? What do you do in these situations? If you're not sure, let me give you some advice from my own life on how to handle these kinds of situations.

When I worked at a car dealership as a salesman, the compensation was salary and non-commission. Some employees were telling me not to clock in, because I was paid on salary; and, others told me to clock in. It was very confusing, and I was trying to figure it out. When I clocked in, I was getting paid. This taught me that sometimes people give you wrong information; if you have questions, even answers, you need to verify that the information you're given is correct.

In the next example, I told somebody to do something and they did not do it. At the job, if you wanted to switch shifts with another coworker you must let a manager know that you are switching shifts. So, I told my coworker to let my manager know and he didn't tell him.

You need to find people that are reliable. Being reliable is a good trait to have in the work place; it will improve your performance on the job.

Why do you need to be reliable?

One reason is so people can trust you. A business, or person, that has a reputation of being reliable will have repeat business. When you are reliable in your job, you likely will have less supervision and you will have more responsibility. Just be on the lookout for people who try to take advantage of you and your trustworthiness.

CHAPTER 6

TRAINING FOR SUCCESS

Life is precious. Some people get to the end of their life only to realize that they never really lived. Life is not just about working to pay rent or waiting for the weekend.

Do you regret things you didn't do? If you are reading this book, then you still have an opportunity to make changes. If you are serious about achieving the things you want, then you need to be serious about training.

Many people *kind of want* a career change. If you *kind of want* things in life, then you will *kind of get* the results you want. Find that thing that ignites your spark!

Life is should be full of evaluation and training. Evaluation is necessary to be able to see your effectiveness, but you must train to be better. To determine the right training, you need to know what kind of training you need. The preparation process is not complete without a plan for evaluation. You must see your life as a training ground, that way you will be able to handle whatever comes your way.

Training can be made by the current situations and of the possible changes coming. When the evaluation is systematic it is more defensible. The evaluation must measure range of things in life that you may need to know about. One of the first consideration must be to determine the purpose for which training is needed. Another good reason for evaluation is to validate any guessing. Figure out if training is helping your employees if you're in management.

One way to be successful in your life is to follow instructions from an instructor. An instructor can design a test to determine whether an individual has certain level of skills. Without test how could instructors judge the effectiveness of an individual.

Test have value to the instructor primarily in determining the extent to which employees are meeting the objectives of a unit instruction. To provide information that helps in decision making it is necessary that the test represent a comprehensive sample of the important material in the lesson.

Test help to provide instructors with clues about the value of what is taught and what is emphasized. When instructors look carefully at the content of the test, they can see what subject matter they can consider is important. Many instructors do not realize what values, they have with respect to the specialties until they see what they place value in their test.

Test have a lot of value to managers because they assist in preparing reports on the effectiveness of activities. Organizations that are responsible for training must establish a reputation for employing and maintaining qualified employees.

The first step in planning a test is to outline the objectives. The next step in the learning process is the measurement of progress. In that process find out what weakness do your employees have.

I will share with you about performance testing.

The objective of all employee's development is to train the employee to do something new. One of the purposes of training is to create in employees the ability to put knowledge into practice on the job, the degree of skilled acquired needs to be measured.

Practice application and work hard is important. If a new machine operator is expected to run equipment properly, he or she must have opportunities to operate the machine. The need for success in real situations dictates the need for tryout experiences before the real one takes place.

CHAPTER 7

Examples of Humility

One of the most powerful character traits one can have is to be humble. but, what does that mean?

One definition of being humble is "showing a modest or low state of one's own importance." To be humble actually is far greater than that.

To me, being humble means being last in line, not first. It is the ability to control your emotions under any circumstances. It is listening more than talking. It is the ability to let go of pride, which is hard for most people.

Throughout this chapter, I will give offer advice on how to develop humility, share stories of people that showed humility, and give scenarios of my life where I had to be humble.

Sam Walton, the founder of Wal-mart told the story of how these people from Brazil called him and wanted him to share his secrets. They sent letters to other "big box" stores but only Sam Walton responded. The Brazilians came to America and, when they arrived, Sam Walton picked them up – but not in a Lamborghini.

They all sat down at the table at Sam Walton's place. Now you think since they came over to see Mr. Walton, the Brazilians would be asking the questions, but it was the opposite. Sam Walton was asking them how he could make his stores better. He humbled himself to learn from them. Sam Walton learned from others. Being humble is the ability to ask questions–even if you already know the answer. Michael Jordan humbled himself many times to listen to others. I love holding the doors for people to let them in. When I was in line to buy food, I would let people skip me, so they could pay for their items. You have to see yourself being a student for life and never graduated. A student has to continue to learn and always ask their teacher questions.

Here are some tips to being humble:

1. Ask for feedback

2. Confront your prejudice

3. Ask yourself questions

4. Ask others questions

5. Say "I'm sorry"

Examples of Humility

6. Don't say "I know it all"

7. Don't let others offend you

Humility involves an outlook that is other-oriented rather than self-focused. Ask several close friends to be honest about certain things, like areas where you need to grow. Here are some attributes of a humble person:

1. A humble person can always ask for help and they do not insist that everything being done their way.

2. They are quick to forgive others; they are also difficult to offend.

3. They are very patient and do not get frustrated with the weakness of others.

4. They know when to be quiet and listen.

5. They easily admit mistakes.

6. Humble people don't want accolades or praise.

7. Humble leaders treat everyone with respect.

Applying humility at work

Here are some tips for working with management.

1. Be proactive and request a 1-on-1 meeting with your manager.

2. Say "To be the best, I want to learn from the best." Let management know how much you appreciate them for helping you.

3. Ask your manager how you can develop to make more contributions to the company.

What affect will humility have on your life?

Humility will make you a better leader. It will set you up for success from learning from others. You will be able to share your vision with successful people. As a leader, you want to be able to have humility when you start your own business so you can set a clear direction for your employees.

Humility will let you know that you can utilize your strength. You will grow as a leader. Start listening to successful people in business.

Would you look to someone for guidance and leadership if they did not truly care about your goals? Of course not! Great leaders are not just focused on getting group members to finish task, they have genuine passion and enthusiasm. Let people know that you care about their progress.

To be humble maintain a good attitude. With a positive attitude, you are looking at the good side of things. People are attracted to you when you have a positive attitude.

Let's face it everyone has made mistakes. As leader you need to learn from your mistakes.

Examples of Humility

Can you be humble and confident at the same time? Yes! Being confident can attract people, but some people may find it boastful. Therefore, you want to be humble and know that you are confident in what you can accomplish. Many times, people mistake humility for weakness. So, when you are growing in humility, do not let people take advantage of you. Becoming a Better Listener

One reason people fail in this life is because they refuse to be humble and listen. Do you want to master the art of listening? If you tend to zone out when someone is talking to you or notice that people do not often chose you as their confidant, it's time to start practicing this skill. Taking an active approach to listening will approve your relationships and will enrich your self-confidence.

When someone is talking to you give them your full attention. Do not have your cell phone out. Try to put yourself in someone else's shoes. Have empathy toward the person talking. Try to understand that person. Seek common ground.

Many find it hard to concentrate during a conversation because they feel self-conscious about how they appear to the other person. Part of being a good listener is having the ability to stop thinking about yourself.

Use body language as a way to express to someone that you are paying attention. When you are leaning forward during a face-to-face conversation, this shows that you are interested in hearing more. Make eye contact when you are having a conversation. Nod your head for acknowledgment. Do not fidget or slouch Make sure your body language conveys interest–not boredom. If you are busy picking your nails, tapping your feet, crossing your arms or leaning your head on your hand someone might end the conversation quick.

Sit up straight to show that you are engaged in the conversation. React to words in a positive way by smiling or laughing.

Ask questions. This keeps people talking and indicates you have been listening.

Who should you take advice from? Who should you listen to? This can depend on what it is. If you are trying to start a business, and you need good advice, you should probably take advice from a business person vs somebody who is not a business person. You also want to be careful of what kind of advice you want to take from business people. Why do we have people in America that never started a business before and want to tell somebody else how to run a business. In my opinion that is not a smart idea.

If you want to learn about eating healthy, I would suggest you take advice from a nutritionist. There is a difference between listen and taking advice. You can learn from somebody but not take their advice.

CHAPTER 8

STUCK IN NEUTRAL

Have you ever been stuck in life–feeling like you're not making progress?

If you are having trouble moving forward, perhaps this is a good chance to do some reflecting. To start, look back and reflect on what has happened in your life. It's a good idea to write down your thoughts.

In what areas did you have success – big or small?

Who helped you when you needed help?

What motivated you to push yourself to be better?

Is there someone that you need to forgive?

There have been times in my life where I was stuck and didn't know what to do. So, I started to think about my past and any success I had. When I reflected on my athletic success in high school, I found the confidence and strength to keep moving forward.

I looked back to see what I was good at. Remember where you were back then and what you can become in the future. Getting a Boost from Mentors

I worked at a lot of jobs in the past where successful people taught me many things. I used to work for a company called My Fit Foods. There was a man (named Jae Pae) who was district manager at Fitness Connection and area director for My Fit Foods. He (Jae Pae) was also the CEO of Results Camp. This manager motivated me to read more books and gave me advice about how to be successful. As a result of taking his advice, I was ranked No. 1 in the nation in my position at My Fit Foods for four consecutive months. If you need direction in your life, think back on how people helped you.

Pushing Yourself

What do you do when you don't feel like moving forward? Maybe it's time to redefine. To "redefine" means to "reexamine or to define something again differently." Redefining yourself is a tactic you can use when you are stalled out. "Redefine: To define something again differently."

When you reexamine the things that made you happy, you can be motivated by it. When you reexamine the things that went wrong in your life, you can learn from it. What can you change about yourself that can make your life better? When you are driving a car, you sometimes need to adjust your route to accommodate the circumstances. Have you made any recent adjustments in your life? What are you doing to push yourself?

Shifting Gears

Find out what you need to adjust. Are you a person that goes to bed late? Are you not eating right? Ask yourself "What can I do differently that would take me in a better direction?"

Adjusting takes some time; but, it's a good opportunity to get to know yourself better. Find out what you really like and don't like. You will have to search to learn what you need to move forward. You can do this!

Still need motivation?

One day at work, a coworker said, "Kaleb, I feel like something is missing in my life." I had previously learned about myself that when I felt that something was missing, I would treat myself to something new.

Some people work really hard but never reward themselves. When you reward yourself, it boosts your self-esteem. It acknowledges your accomplishments. So, let me ask: What is new in your life? Maybe it's time to treat yourself to something new. Once you do, set a new goal and reward yourself when you achieve it.

Another thing you can do is find people that can boost your confidence that will allow you to see things from a better perspective. It may be a friend or a coworker that you work with.

Are you an introvert? Maybe it is time for you to get out of your comfort zone. Step up and step out and start taking the initiative to get things done. If you are shy, you can learn to be more social. Join a networking group for a topic that you are comfortable with and meet new people. Memorize an "elevator pitch" so that you control the first thing you say. If you don't have an elevator pitch, it's simple to create one. (An elevator pitch is a quick summary of what you do; something you could say in an elevator ride with a stranger.) Write down one to two sentences that describe you: either your personality, your interests or your best skill. As an example, the editor of this book has an elevator pitch that goes like this: "I edit books for aspiring and published authors." That's it. Short and sweet, but complete. Practice writing a few different ideas until you find a concise elevator pitch that best sums you up. Then, when asked by others to describe yourself, the shyness fades as you state your pitch with confidence. And, always smile when you meet people. Practice smiling when you talk on the phone. It really makes a difference.

Earlier I was talking about having confidence. I started to have confidence many years ago when I was in high school. I was good at sports and I became team captain. After school I started jobs where I was required to sell products. Work helped me develop confidence to talk to people.

I became very comfortable talking to people and now I find it easy. You must start somewhere to build your confidence. My confidence grew when I was working in the fitness industry. As mentioned in Chapter X, when I was working at the gym, people that didn't have a membership tried to sneak in and I had to tell them you cannot work out without a membership. That made me uncomfortable for a while because I wanted to avoid conflict.

What made me tough was how I handled criticism. I started to learn from people criticizing me. When criticized, some people get upset and feel victimized.

To avoid this, you have to start sticking up for yourself in a respectful way. This will take practice and time and will be a growing process for many. Every day might be different but stay prepared for it. With practice, it can make you mentally sharp to handle the pressure.

Forward Thinking Are you looking to make things better for your future? What drives you to do your best? One way people fail in life financially is because they fail to make a profit.

Many people work for a pay check but do not work for their future. Many people do not invest money. Many people do not invest time. They make excuses about things that could help them in the future.

Many times, I've invited people to seminars, but they offer an excuse as to why they can't attend. Successful people don't make excuses, and they do make time for their future. They learn things from other people to make themselves better. Many people live their lives daily without making any progress towards their future—especially in their finances.

Many people procrastinate because they don't have their priorities right. The future is uncertain, so you must be prepared. One way to prepare is to work different jobs to learn different skills. I worked as a business representative for a company that provided accounting, tax and bookkeeping services. Why? Because I planned to start my own business, so I needed to learn about taxes and bookkeeping. In another job working for a roofing company, I was required to knock on homeowner's doors. This requirement enhances my communication skills AND, as a future homeowner, I learned a lot about insurance for roofing repairs and replacements.

When you take the time to learn, it only pays off if you apply what you've learned. Are you making an effort to learn something new that can benefit your future? We all have the same 24 hours in a day. Start somewhere, even at your current place of employment. Ask to try something new or offer to help on a project that's not directly yours. This will build your credibility with your managers. Figure out what works for you.

When you apply for a job, the hiring company will ask you for a resumé. They will look at your job history to see what you did. If you have credibility, they will hire you. A good way to recognize if you have good credibility is to ask yourself: Do your friends think well of you?

Are you known for getting things done right? If not, then it's a good idea to start learning now. You can start by trying to help and motivate people. You might have something of value that no one else has. It is good to work on yourself because it will put you in a place to help people.

I learned a lot about how people think when I sold cars. When you understand how people think, you can guide them better. I also had to understand people's needs. It made me develop sincerity for customers that really needed a car. I went the extra mile to get a lot of things done for people. When I worked for the accounting firm, my job was to go to a business and ask if we can save them money on their taxes. I met a lot of entrepreneurs who were not aware of how much taxes they were supposed to pay. Some businesses were struggling because they were paying too much taxes. A thrift store owner told me her struggles, which led to us being able to find a solution that involved affordable bookkeeping.

In that job, I learned a lot about business, people and how to help business owners grow their businesses.

When you start your own business there is on-going learning. It is good to have a mindset of being a problem-solver. Solving problems is a great skill to have for yourself, somebody else or for a company. Ask yourself: Can I provide a service to somebody? What do I know that could help people?

Create opportunities for yourself by working on personal development. You can start by reading books or find a mentor. Find a way that works for you, but start taking action. Do not procrastinate. Do not put things off that you know are important. Put in the effort to get things done. If you get tired, do not quit–you'll miss the pay off. You can overcome all the roadblocks in your life to get where you want to be.

Here are some of my accomplishment was freshmen of the year in basketball. I was the number 1 performer at a nutrition retail store in my position. I have won 4 public speaking awards.

When I was selling cars as a car salesman, I was very consistent in numbers over all. I started my own real estate business. I also have four certificates from currency trading. This is only some of my achievements. This was hard work, but I kept going and I kept learning.

CHAPTER 9

SHOULD YOU GO ALONE?

When you want to achieve things in your life, you have a choice: Do you want to pursue the goal by yourself, or do you want someone to help you? First, determine what you want to have success in and, then, determine if you will need help getting there.

As you strive for success, you will come across people that are going to give you guidance. At the same time, you must be cautious and make sure their guidance is the correct way to go.

You must know the motive behind the person who is helping you. You do not want to have someone help you that is going to double cross you. Get to know that person first and see if he or she could be a mentor for you. This might take some time. People will come and go in your life, and not everybody is going to be your friend. Not everybody needs to know about what you are doing. It is not a good idea to share your business ideas with everyone you talk to.

It will be a good idea to choose the right kind of friends to have with you on your journey. I would advise you to pay close attention to your friends if you are considering asking them to help you start a business. What if you have a nice business idea but you tell the wrong person and they steal your idea? Have you ever thought about that before?

Another option is to keep your business ideas to yourself. If this is your path, it will be up to you to decide on which way to go. For me, I have told people that I am starting a business, but I never told anyone my idea(s). I know that I have something valuable and I will not let my treasure be dug up by somebody else.

You also must consider that by not getting help, you could miss out on great advice, mentoring and opportunity. It's a tough choice, but it's your decision to make. There are many ways to sort this out; you just have to be willing to invest time and patience.

I went to a lot of business seminars and I met many people. I had to see what kind of people I wanted in my circle that are entrepreneurs. I needed to know what kind of people I wanted on my team. It's like in football: coaches have to select the right players because football is a team game. A coach must know how each player performs at his best; it's why they hold practice. Not everybody will get chance to be on the team because the coach will make decisions on whom to keep. Every season, professional football coaches make adjustments to the team. As the head coach of your own business journey, you will have to make adjustments from time to time, too. The more people you know, the more networking events you attend, the more you read, the better your business choices will be.

Sometimes, you may need to let go of people that don't motivate you or who try to distract you from your goals. Surround yourself with people that motivate you.

If you take the path of pursuing your goals alone, then invest the time to learn. At some point, you must make decisions for yourself. Do you want to be a leader? If so, you need to know that you will have to make decisions that will change the outcome for the better or for the worse. If you go alone, beware that you will probably face critics. People will put pressure on you to do things. You will be put on the spot. Are you ready to get in that driver's seat?

How are you preparing to be an entrepreneur? This will be something you need to figure out on your own. Business owners must be prepared to adjust because of supply and demand. They make decisions based on what consumers want. You will face tough, uncomfortable decisions. You might make decisions that you regret later but are valuable learning experiences.

One way you can determine a decision is to count the cost beforehand. You need to ask yourself if the decision will hurt you, your employees or your business, or if it will make things better. If the outcome is bad, then you must develop a plan to recover from it; then find a way not to make the same mistake. Life will continue to go on this is way; you have been prepared for anything that could happen.

CHAPTER 10

Respect Along the Way

What does it mean to respect another person?

What does "respect" mean? When we understand what "respect" means, then we are better able to provide it.

Respect in the Hebrew language is the word "masso," which means "lifting [another person] up." The word "nata" is another Hebrew word which means "to lift, carry, to take," according to Strong's Exhaustive Concordance.

The word respect also has a Latin background; the Latin verb for "respect" is the word "respicere," which means "to look back at, regard." In modern English, respect also means "reverence." Merriam-Webster defines it as "to recognize the worth of a person or thing." Respect can also mean a feeling of admiration for something or someone elicited by their abilities, qualities or achievements.

How do we really respect someone? Learning what respect is will allow you to grow in maturity and it will teach you how to treat other people right.

When you want to be respectful, try to put yourself in someone else's shoes. Respect deals with showing that you value another person's perspective, experience and space.

Showing Respect

Being kind and having common courtesy is important. Being respectful starts with an understanding of considering other people's feelings. Ask yourself how you would want to be treated in a given situation and treat other people that way.

Being Polite: Manners vs. Etiquette

What's the difference, you ask? The concepts of etiquette and good manners seem pointless when you are a kid, but when you grow up you soon realize that these customary functions keep our society running smoothly. Practicing good manners is a way to be respectful of other people; it shows a kind heart and consideration for others. There are many social circumstances, like eating in a restaurant, waiting in line, or navigating traffic, that require we exercise social etiquette, which are accepted and orderly ways of doing things. Without manners, there'd be little kindness. Without etiquette, there'd be constant chaos.

How to be polite

Put your phone away during a meeting, even if it's a casual get-together when you're trying to get know someone. This shows that you respect that person's time and that they have your complete attention.

Wait your turn and do not to cut in line at a store.

It's not good to "cut people off" in traffic. People have lost their lives when they became angry at another driver. Road rage is real.

Do not discriminate against people. Be respectful to everyone, not just the people you know. Many people show respect for those upon whom they want to make a good impression; but, then are rude to others. There is truth in the saying: You can judge the character of others by how they treat those who can do nothing for them.

Always be kind

Being kind to all people is an ultimate expression of respect. For example, homeless people are often overlooked or treated rudely, but they deserve the same respect and courtesy as your neighbor. The differences among us are what makes life interesting; and, you probably have more things in common with others than you realize. Even when you really don't understand the other persons' point of view, it's a show of respect to simply be courteous and civil.

Communicating respectfully

Listen when someone is talking to you, when you are having a conversation. Being a good listener is basic sign of respect. If you look bored or if you interrupt the person, you might be coming off not caring for what she or he is saying. Practice listening more intently when you are having a conversation. Think before you speak. When it's your turn to talk try to respond respectfully.

One tip is to know your own limitations: know the topics that you should avoid discussing if you don't know someone very well so you can steer clear of certain questions.

Respecting yourself

You are an important person and you deserve to be treated well. Work on treating yourself right. I would practice empathy and compassion to really understand yourself and other people. You can be courteous even if you don't know the other person very well. Respect stems from a sense of empathy and a deep sense of shared understanding where other people are coming from. Develop a sense of self-respect because it can help you develop healthy relationship and people around you will see you as a person who is worthy of respect. If you do not respect yourself, start working on personal development.

Get to know yourself. The more you understand yourself, the more you appreciate how unique you are. Discover your personality and talents. It can take while to complete this process of self–discovery.

It is important to forgive people if they've wronged you. It is important to forgive yourself as well. Start building your self-confidence. Simple steps are to smile more and say "thank you" when somebody compliments you.

To have respect, you must be aware of the person you really are. If someone gives you helpful and constructive criticism evaluate what they are telling you. It might help you to be a better person. Know the difference when someone tells you something in a nice way and when someone tells you something that is true in harsh way. Evaluate the criticism honestly and carefully. Treat yourself with respect.

Target areas for improvement by taking the time to really think about yourself and consider areas you want to improve. For example, maybe you want to be a better listener. In Chapter X, we discussed how being a good listener can help you to be successful.

How to teach respect

Respect is one of the most important things you can learn in life. A child needs to learn this. A sense of respect is vital to succeeding in school, holding a job and having friends. When it comes to teaching children respect, you need to remember that they naturally look up to their caregivers and oftentimes imitate them. One thing to know for a parent you need to live a life of respect in front your children. If you act disrespectfully to them, they might pick that up. I would encourage activities that require cooperation; they put them in a position to learn how to respect others. Teach children to be honest with themselves when they make mistakes; give them a chance to correct their mistakes. We all make mistakes.

The ultimate question: Is respect given or is it earned?

A lot of people wonder HOW to give respect. Is respect given or is it earned?

When respect is earned, it means you must perform or do something to gain approval in order to be shown respect. When respect is given, it's an expression of another person's worth, regardless of performance.

For example, a car salesman should give respect to his or her customer by being fair and honest. The customer should not have to earn this respect; it should be given. If respect is not given at a car dealership, then neither the salesperson nor the customer will be happy. When I was selling cars, one of my managers put me on the spot and asked if I can close a deal. I said that I could. He gave me the respect to take the lead and close the deal. If a person always feels that respect must be earned, then how can someone have a chance to earn respect if he or she is not given that opportunity?

Giving respect

Giving respect should make us feel self-worth and increase our confidence. If you have a friend that is successful, give him respect by listening to what he has to say. Respect given promotes a positive vibe that people can sense. In return, they often offer you the same respect.

Our military is another good example. Remember, the definition of respect is having a deep admiration for someone or something by their ability, qualities or achievement. Respect should be given to those who serve, or have served, in our military–and those who attempted to join. Every time I see someone in uniform, I thank them for their service. I give respect; and, they've earned it.

I believe that respect is one of the foundations for personal and professional relationships. A person's character needs to be right. Giving respect to others shows the richness of your character in a very genuine manner.

Now, you can become great at what you do! You can be successful if you put in the work. Just keep going forward. I hope you'll take the tips from this book and apply them in your life. It's time for you to go and be somebody!